SCIENCE OF FUN STUFF

Unmasking the Science of Superpowers!

by Jordan D. Brown
illustrated by Scott Burroughs

Ready-to-Read

Simon Spotlight
New York   London   Toronto

SIMON SPOTLIGHT

An imprint of Simon & Schuster Children's Publishing Division

1230 Avenue of the Americas, New York, New York 10020

This Simon Spotlight edition September 2016

For information about special discounts for bulk purchases, please contact Simon & Schuster Special Sales at 1-866-506-1949 or business@simonandschuster.com.

The Simon & Schuster Speakers Bureau can bring authors to your live event. For more information or to book an event contact the Simon & Schuster Speakers Bureau at 1-866-248-3049 or visit our website at www.simonspeakers.com.

Manufactured in the United States of America 0816 LAK

2 4 6 8 10 9 7 5 3 1

Library of Congress Cataloging-in-Publication Data

Names: Brown, Jordan. author. | Burroughs, Scott, illustrator.

Title: Unmasking the science of superpowers! / by Jordan D. Brown ; illustrated by Scott Burroughs.

Other titles: Science of fun stuff.

Description: First edition. | New York : Simon Spotlight, [2016] | Series: Science of fun stuff | Audience: Ages 6-8.? | Audience: K to grade 3.?

Identifiers: LCCN 2015046308| ISBN 9781481467780 (trade paper) | ISBN 9781481467797 (hardcover) | ISBN 9781481467803 (eBook)

Subjects: LCSH: Science—Miscellanea—Juvenile literature. | Superheroes—Miscellanea—Juvenile literature. | Technological innovations—Juvenile literature.

Classification: LCC Q175.2 .B76 2016 | DDC 502—dc23 LC record available at http://lccn.loc.gov/2015046308

CONTENTS

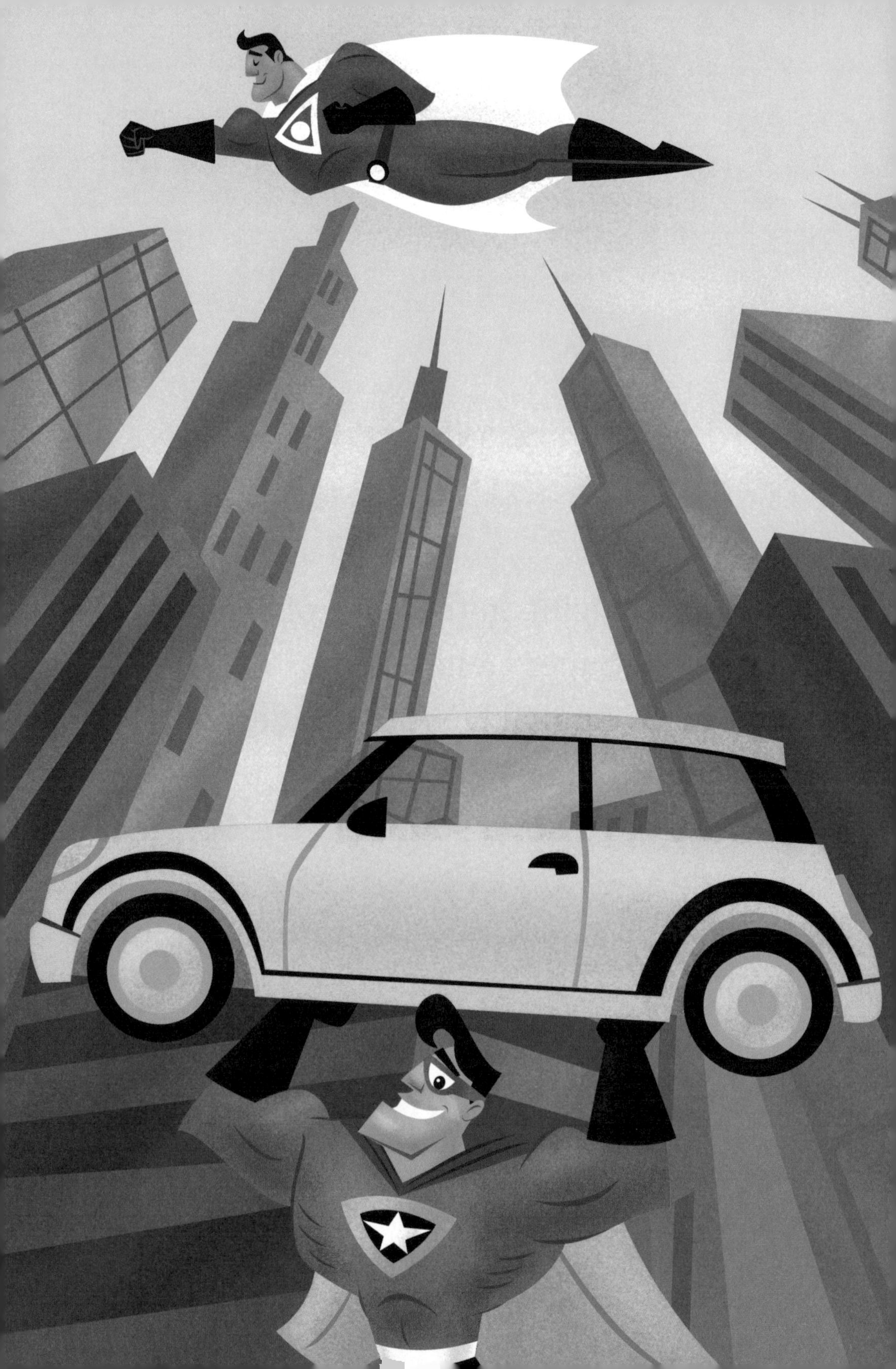

CHAPTER 1
Flying in the Face of Science

Did you ever wish you had superpowers? In movies, TV, and comic books, superheroes do amazing, fantastic things. They can leap across rooftops and fly like a rocket, or run faster than lightning. If someone is trapped under a car—no problem!—they easily lift it. In real life, super feats like these are impossible, right? Not so fast, say scientists. Today's science fiction may someday be science fact.

How, you ask? Every day, scientists and engineers are exploring human biology, studying animal genes, and creating high-tech inventions that may one day give you superpowers. But before we get to that, let's look at how superheroes break laws—scientific laws, that is. A scientific law is a statement that describes something in nature that seems to always be true.

Gravity

When superheroes want to go somewhere, they put up their fists, jump off the ground, and soon they're soaring through the air. If you were to do the same thing, what would happen? (Besides you looking silly.) You would fall back to the ground in seconds. That's because, unlike a superhero, you have to follow the scientific laws of gravity.

In the 1600s supersmart guy Isaac Newton wrote scientific laws about gravity. He observed that gravity is the invisible force that attracts all objects to one another. He also figured out that huge objects, like planet Earth, have much more gravity than smaller objects, like people. That's why we stay down on the ground. Birds and airplanes are also pulled down by Earth's gravity, but they have wings that can glide through the air. Most superheroes don't have wings, so how do they beat Earth's gravity?

Drag

When superheroes zoom through the sky faster than a speeding bullet, they break another scientific law about drag. Drag is just what it sounds like—it slows down any object moving through the air. Drag exists because air is made up of an invisible sea of molecules. When an object moves quickly through the air, the air molecules rub against it. And the faster an object moves, the more air molecules are rubbing against it, increasing drag. How are superheroes able to overcome drag so easily?

Force

When flying superheroes hear someone yell "Help!!!", they take off and—*Whoooooooosh!*—they can be anywhere in an instant. In real life though, nothing moves without a force pushing or pulling it. Another one of Newton's scientific laws, his first law of motion, says just that: A still object will remain still unless some force acts on it. So, what is the force behind a superhero's flying power? Most of them don't have jet engines strapped to their backs.

Superheroes in movies and TV and comic books don't have to follow scientific laws. That's because most of the superheroes we watch or read about have been dreamed up by writers and artists—they can make their superhero characters do whatever they want, even if it's not possible in real life. Science might make superpowers like flight impossible for humans, but people with other kinds of "superpowers" do exist. These people got their unusual abilities from a place inside them—their genes.

CHAPTER 2
Super Genes

It might be strange to think about, but your entire body, from your head to your toes, is made up of trillions of cells. Cells are the supersmall building blocks of all living things. They're so small, in fact, that you would need to use a microscope, a machine for viewing very small objects, to see them.

But if you thought that cells were small, there's something even smaller! Each one of the trillions of cells in your body contains about 20,000 to 25,000 genes. Genes are sets of chemicals that give cells specific instructions about what we look like, what we can do, and how we will grow. Sometimes tiny differences in a person's genes can make them extra strong or fast. But there are limits: No humans have genes that let them fly, turn invisible, or shoot lightning out of their hands.

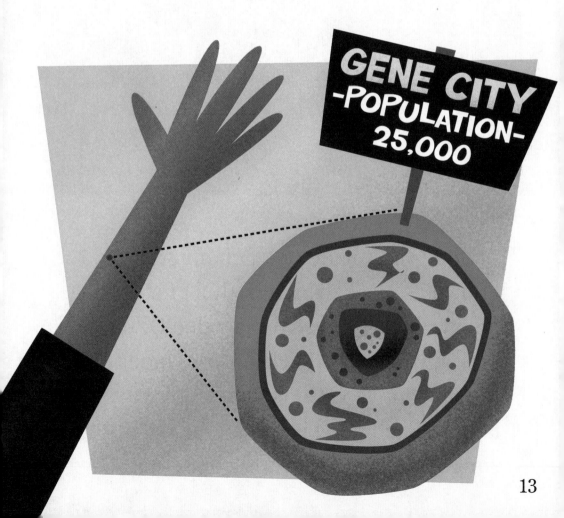

GENE CITY
-POPULATION-
25,000

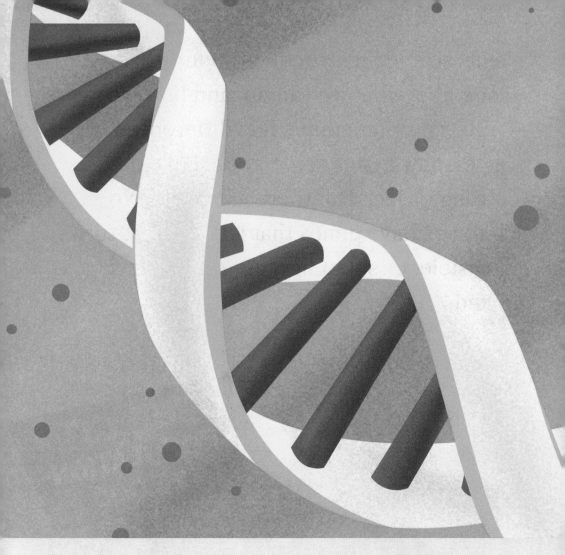

Genes are made up of chemicals known as DNA, which is short for deoxyribonucleic acid (say: dee-OX-ee-rye-bow-new-CLAY-ick A-sid). Under a microscope DNA looks like a long twisted ladder. Each gene is a section, like a set of rungs, on the ladder.

The ladder's rungs are made of different chemicals called bases, which are known by the letters A, T, C, or G. These bases pair up to form a rung on the ladder. Usually A pairs with T, and C pairs with G. The order, or sequence, of these four bases in the ladder tells the cell what to do. One of the genes that helps give a person curly hair might look like ATGCCGTAAT, while one of the genes for having freckles might be GCGCATCGAT.

Some genes contain a few hundred bases, while others are made up of more than two *million* bases. When your body makes new cells, it makes copies of your DNA. And when genes make copies of themselves, they sometimes change, or mutate. Different bases might get paired, for example, or a base might be added or removed.

Scientists call these changes mutations. Some mutations are inherited from your parents, while others might happen randomly, like if your body makes a mistake in copying your DNA. Genes mutate all the time, but that's okay because your DNA will usually repair itself.

Some people are born with very rare mutations that can make them sick. But other even rarer genetic mutations can cause abilities that look like superpowers!

Super Bones

There's a very rare genetic mutation called sclerosteosis (say: sklair-AH-stee-oh-sis) that gives some people very thick, hard-to-break bones. Believe it or not, people with this kind of mutation have survived car crashes without any broken bones. Scientists who study sclerosteosis hope to create medicines for people with very weak bones. Supercool, right?

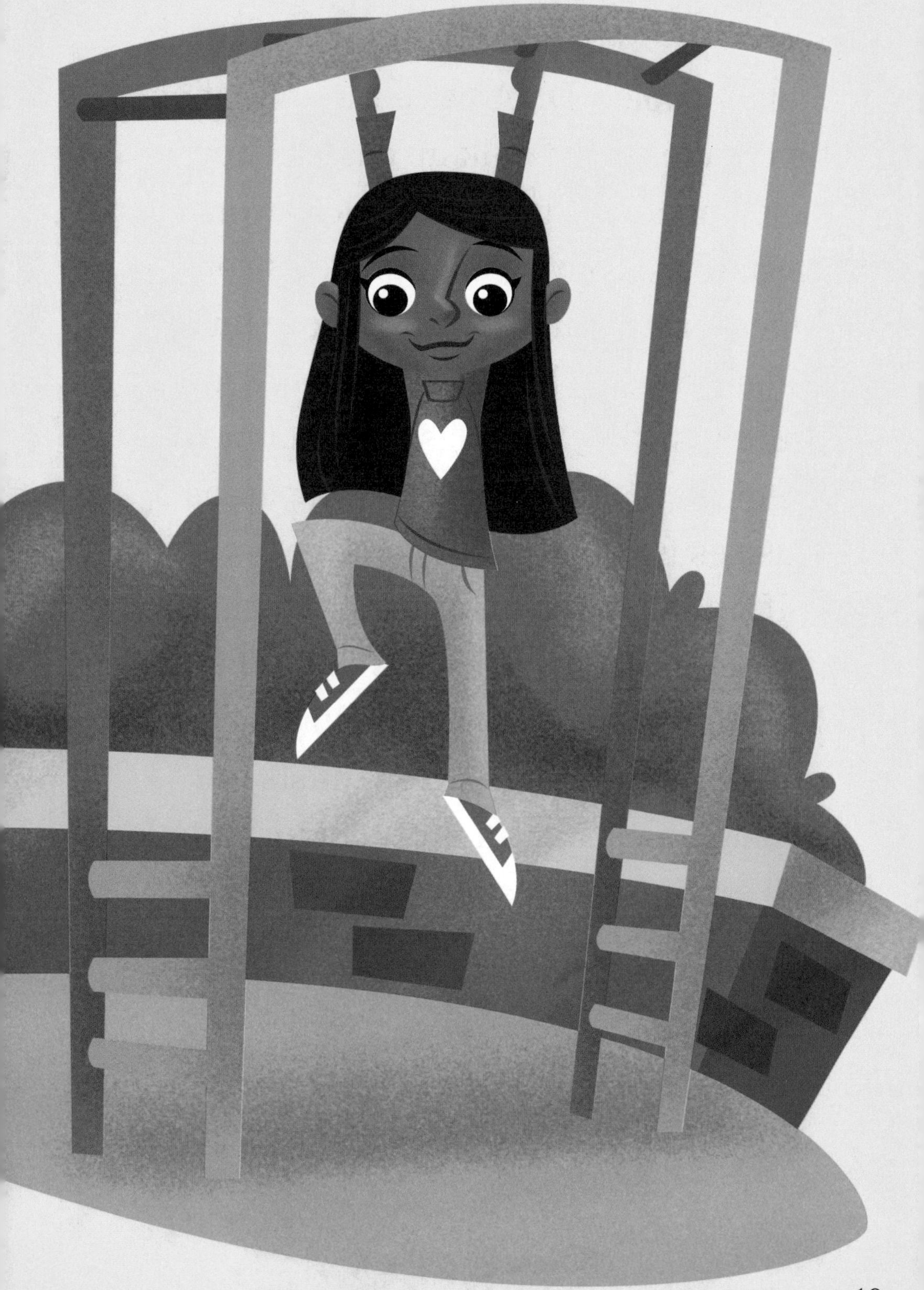

Super Strength

Some people's DNA has a rare mutation that makes them bulk up easily. They develop more muscles with less work than most of us. They're not quite as strong as superheroes, but they have more muscular bodies, even as babies. This extra power is because they have less myostatin, a chemical that normally stops a person's muscles from growing too large.

If a person is born without the gene for myostatin, their bodies have no off switch when it comes to muscle making. Their muscles keep growing. Scientists are hoping to learn from this genetic mutation to treat muscle-weakening diseases.

Super Blood

Some lucky people are born with a rare mutation that gives them extra energy. This gene mutation causes their bodies to make more red blood cells. And the more red blood cells you have, the more oxygen the cells can carry to different parts of the body. This extra oxygen means a big boost of energy—something very important to many athletes, like distance runners. Though it would also be a huge help to superheroes who need extra energy in a fight!

CHAPTER 3
Animal DNA to the Rescue

Humans aren't the only animals with extraordinary talents. Lots of superheroes get their powers from the animal world. Comic book writers know that many creatures already have the superpowers we want. Let's check out some animals that have abilities we'd like to borrow.

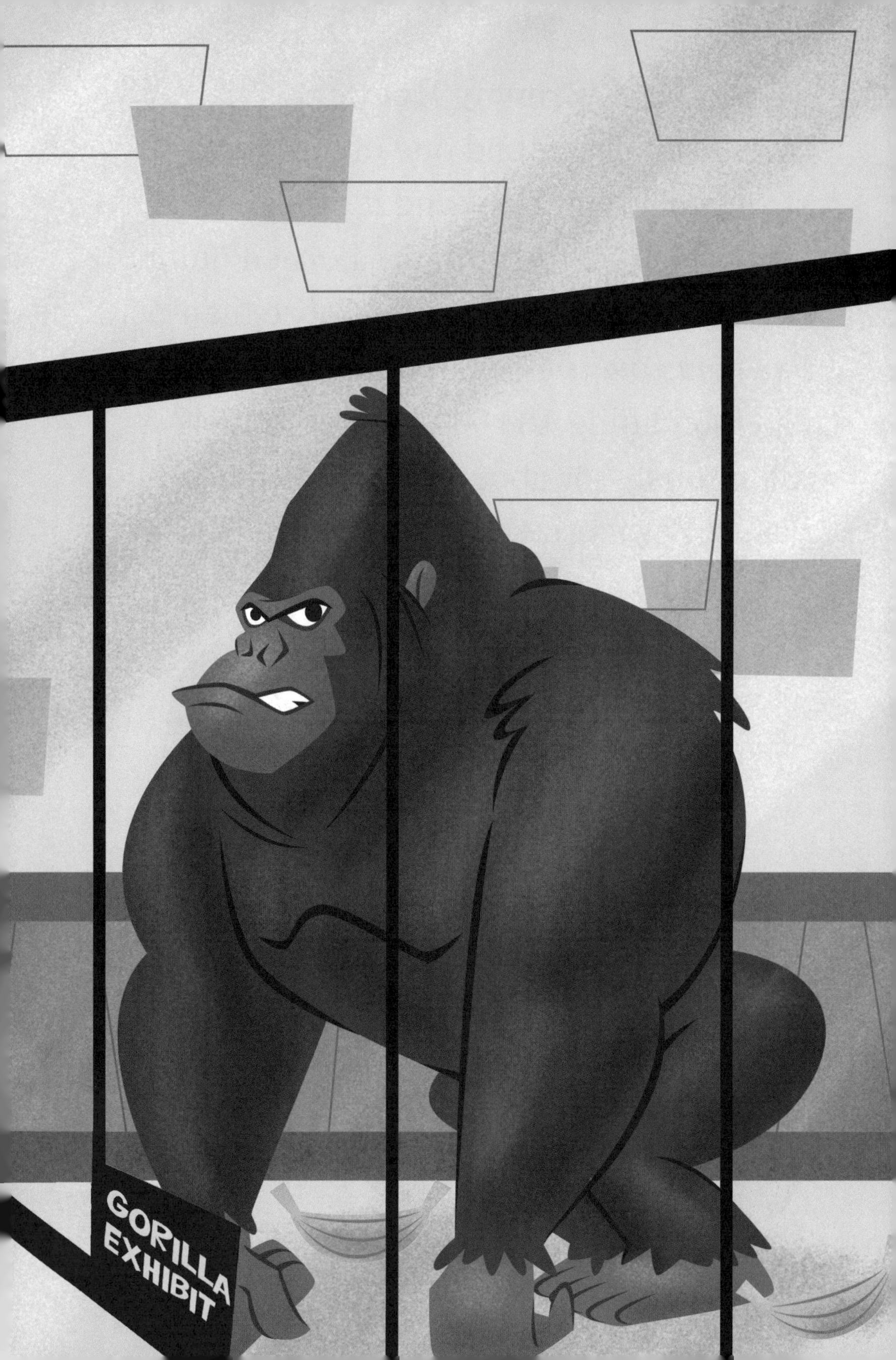
GORILLA
EXHIBIT

Brawny Beetle

Scientists have found one of the world's strongest creatures—and it eats poop for power! That's right, the horned dung beetle is so strong it can lift more than *one thousand times its weight*. That's like a person lifting 180,000 pounds (81,647 kilograms)—or about six double-decker buses! For its size, it is a powerhouse.

Smash! Crash! Pow!

For pure punching power, the go-to creature is the peacock mantis shrimp. This colorful crustacean can whip out its front claws faster than a bullet. And its punch can crash through clamshells for its meals. What's even cooler? Scientists are developing bulletproof, lightweight body armor based on the shell around the mantis shrimp's club arm!

Captain Camouflage

In the bays of Indonesia lurks an eight-armed master of disguise. The mimic octopus can change its color and shape to imitate a slew of underwater creatures. One minute it looks like a sea snake, then—*BAM!*—it resembles a lionfish. You get the idea. All this shape-shifting isn't for fun and games, though: It's about self-defense.

Living Forever

Death? No thanks! A tiny type of jellyfish has the amazing ability to live forever . . . sometimes. The immortal jellyfish does something weird when in danger. If it is starving or injured, this jellyfish can basically age backward. The jellyfish's cells can turn into hundreds of perfect copies of the original baby jellyfish, which then grow up all over again!

Lost Leg, No Problem!

When a salamander gets in a fight, it often lets its enemy bite off a tail or leg. This isn't a big deal because salamanders have the power to regrow body parts. Sounds incredible, right? It's true. After a salamander's leg is lost, cells called macrophages go to work. These cells are part of the immune system. Over time they recreate all the cells to make the leg good as new. Scientists are looking for ways to alter human DNA so that we, too, can regrow body parts if they are lost.

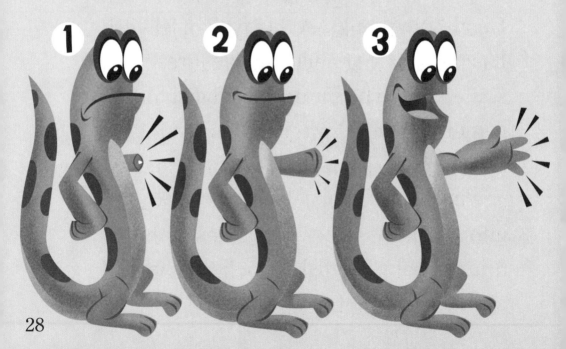

Gutsy Fighters

The sea cucumber might look like a big helpless sausage on the ocean floor, but it has some cool powers. When threatened, it squeezes its organs out of its butt! Predators eat these organs while the sea cucumber escapes. Later, the sea cucumber regrows these lost body parts. That's not all: The sea cucumber's skin can change from solid to liquid by absorbing water. Scientists have created special kinds of plastics based on sea cucumber skin that doctors use in brain operations.

Walking Up Walls

Wouldn't you love to climb buildings with your bare hands? It's a breeze if you're a gecko. These lizards have special hairs on their feet that allow them cling to walls and ceilings. How does this work? Their sturdy hairs create a special electric attraction that makes them stick to surfaces they walk on. Inspired by gecko feet, scientists have already created special rubber hand pads that help people climb walls.

Itty Bitty Bears

Don't be fooled by their cute nickname: "water bears." Tardigrades are eight-legged creatures smaller than a poppy seed, but they are super tough. They can live in boiling water, solid ice, extreme pressure, and even in outer space. The secret to their survival is they can dry out their bodies and slow down their metabolism using a process called cryptobiosis (krip-toe-bye-OH-sis). When they are returned to water—sometimes years later—they come alive again. Water bears have been on Earth for more than five hundred million years, and we expect them to be around for five hundred million more!

CHAPTER 4
Super Gadgets

Borrowing DNA from other animals is an exciting idea, but scientists are still researching. Meanwhile, engineers are inventing cool machines to boost human abilities. Engineers (say: en-jin-EARS) are people with scientific training who plan, design, and build things. While scientists focus on understanding nature and the universe, engineers focus on solving problems by making new systems, products, and machines. They might ask, "How can I help humans become stronger?" or "How can I make an airplane fly faster?"

The answers to these questions
are pretty super! Some of the mighty
machines engineers are creating blur
the line between robot and person. In
this chapter you'll see how engineers are
pushing the limits of science by creating
gadgets to help people run faster, lift more
weight, and even fly.

Super Suits

Many superheroes get their powers from high-tech super suits that make them superstrong and superfast. Could anything like this really happen? Engineers are developing super suits called robotic exoskeletons that give users increased strength. Researchers at Tokyo University created a "muscle suit" to make it easier for nurses to carry their patients.

These super suits have another important use—helping paralyzed people walk again. All someone has to do is shift their balance, and the sensors in the suit move their legs forward.

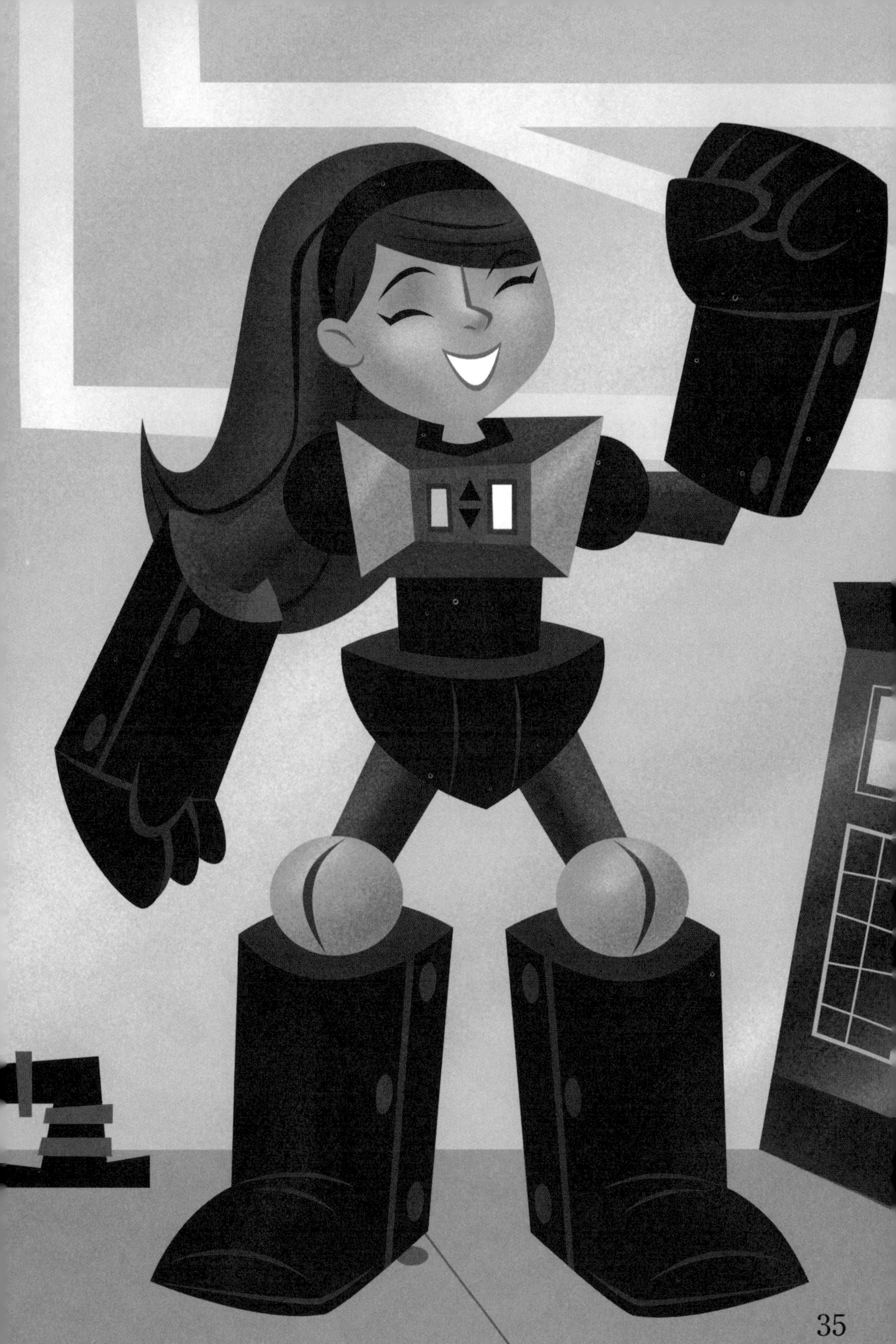

Up, Up, and Away

Looking for a high-tech gadget that can help you fly like a superhero? A jetpack is a machine that you strap onto your back. It releases gasses at high speeds to lift you up into the air. While jetpacks are common in sci-fi stories, our technology isn't quite as advanced yet. One big problem is that people are heavy. It takes a lot force to lift a person in the air for longer than a few minutes. While we wait for jetpack technology to take off, there is a fun alternative—the water-powered jetpack. These jetpacks are attached to a boat with a hose.

After strapping on their jetpack, the user squeezes the hand controls to release powerful jets of water from two nozzles on their back. Remember Newton's first law of motion? The water jets push against the surface of the water, causing the user to fly upward at more than twenty miles per hour. The catch? Since the jetpack is attached to the boat, the user can only fly as far as their hose will take them.

Mind Control

Some superheroes have the dazzling power of telekinesis: They can make objects move with their minds. In real life, scientists are figuring out ways to imitate this ability for people who are paralyzed, unable to use their arms or legs. Some researchers have even begun figuring out ways to reconnect a person's brain to their limbs.

How does it work? A tiny computer sensor is implanted in a person's brain. The sensor picks up the electrical pulses of their brain and sends them to a computer. These messages move the motor of a robotic arm.

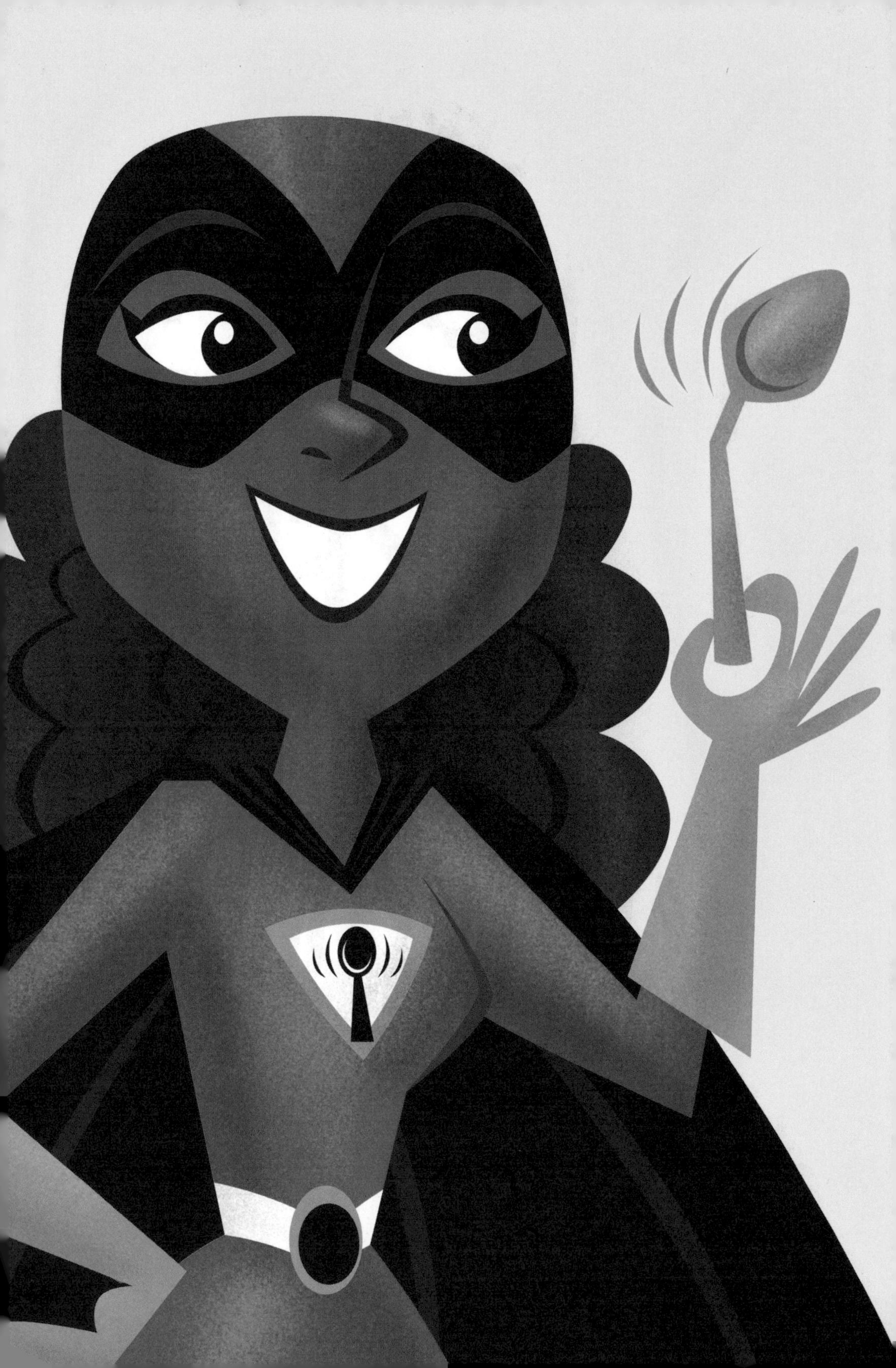

EXPERT HISTORY OF FUN STUFF EXPERT ON SUPERPOWERS!

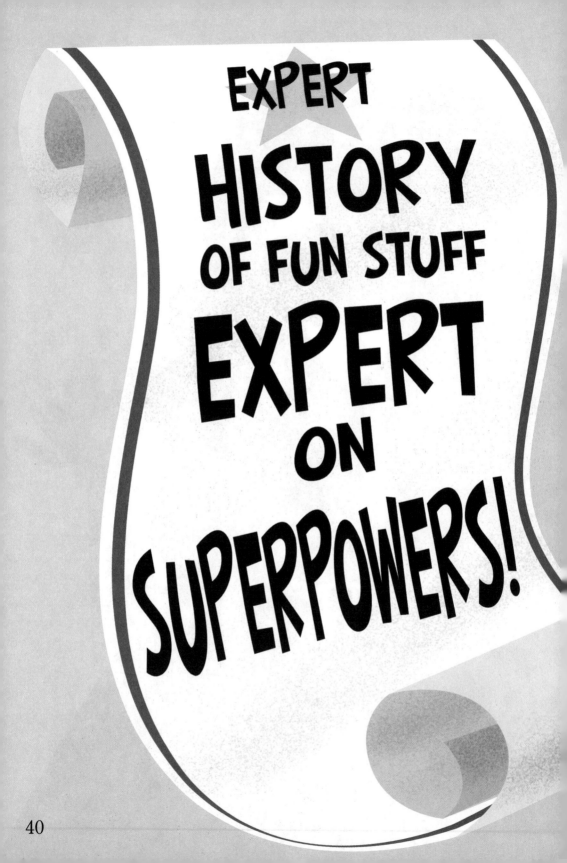

Congratulations! Faster than a speeding bullet, you've come to the end of this book. You're now an official Science of Fun Stuff Expert on superpowers. The next time you see a superhero at the movies or in a comic book, you can think about how their heroic exploits might really happen someday!

Hey, kids! Now that you're an expert on the science of superpowers, turn the page to learn even more about this super subject and some math, language arts, and science along the way!

Super . . . Math?

You would probably be surprised to learn that math factors into many superhero storylines. Anytime a superhero *doubles* their strength, it means they're multiplying their strength by two. And anytime a supervillain has a machine that *halves* a superhero's speed, it means they're dividing their speed by two. Take a look at this superhero story and see how we can tell this same story in a different way with numbers!

Sarah Slothwood is walking down the street, when a car goes whizzing by her head! In a flash Sarah grabs her magic charm and transforms into Speedy Cheetah Lady: a superfast superhero! She peeks around the corner and finds her nemesis, Robotarah, throwing another car right at her, but Sarah dodges the car easily. You see, Sarah's magic charm multiplies her normal human speed—fifteen miles per hour—by ten! In a flash Sarah has Robotarah beaten.

How can we express this story in numbers? Sarah's normal human speed is fifteen miles per hour. But Sarah's magic charm, which transforms her into Speedy Cheetah Lady, multiplies her speed by ten. So we can tell this story by saying:

$$15 \times 10 = 150$$

That means Speedy Cheetah Lady can run one hundred and fifty miles per hour. That's superfast! Can you think of another superhero story that can be expressed using numbers?

Parts of a Story

All great superhero stories have one thing in common . . .
well, five things, actually! These are the five main
parts of a story: characters, setting, plot, conflict, and
resolution.

Characters

This part is easy. A character is anyone in your story:
heroes, villains, ordinary people, even your pet squid!

Setting

The setting is where your story takes place. Setting
usually includes both the time and place, for example—
New York City, 1945.

Plot

This is where things get exciting. The plot is what happens in your story. Everything from getting a glass of water to locking up a bad guy can be considered plot.

Conflict

Conflict is the central problem of your story. Your problem can be a villain on the loose, a tsunami threatening a city, or even that Speedy Cheetah Lady forgot her friend Mighty Badger Dude's birthday!

Resolution

This is how the conflict is solved. For example, Speedy Cheetah Lady could use her superspeed to get Mighty Badger Dude a birthday gift in time for his party.

Can you put all five of these pieces together to make your own superhero story?

Could I do that?

It's no coincidence: Many of our favorite comic book superheroes have secret identities as scientists and engineers. In fact, many of them got their powers from science experiments or by creating cool gadgets in their labs. Want to know what real scientists do each day?

Research Geneticist

Research geneticists (say: jen-ET-ih-sists) study all kinds of things, but they are always looking at how traits are passed down from one generation to the next. They might look at genetic mutations in people to help shed light on a rare disease, or they might develop a special type of strawberry plant that bugs don't want to eat.

Zoologist

Zoologists (zoo-OL-uh-jists) study living things and their environments. As a zoologist you might teach and research for a university, take care of animals at a zoo, or protect animals that are endangered. If you love animals, this might just be the job for you!

Robotics Engineer

Want to play with robots all day? Robotics engineers design and build robots. They also create the programming that allows robots to do their jobs. Because of the time it takes to build a robot and hone its skills, many robotics engineers only work on a few different robots in their entire careers. But the robots they make are very important: Robots can help make things easier and safer for humans.

Being an expert on something means you can get an awesome score on a quiz on that subject! Take this

SCIENCE OF SUPERPOWERS QUIZ
to see how much you've learned.

1. A scientific law describes something in nature that always seems to be . . .
   a. glittery
   b. true
   c. annoying

2. When did Sir Isaac Newton write about gravity?
   a. 1600s
   b. 1923
   c. 2013

3. What do we call the supersmall building blocks of all living things?
   a. amoebas
   b. badgers
   c. cells

4. How many kinds of chemicals, called bases, are there in a gene?
   a. four
   b. seventeen
   c. sixty

5. A change that occurs when a gene copies itself is called a . . .
   a. chemical
   b. mutation
   c. waffle

6. Sclerosteosis is a genetic mutation that causes people to have very strong . . .
   a. hunger
   b. test scores
   c. bones

7. What are the special kinds of cells that help salamanders regrow lost legs and tails?
   a. macrophages
   b. flowers
   c. magnets

8. How do the special hairs on a gecko's feet allow them to stick to surfaces?
   a. They're magical.
   b. They create a sticky goo.
   c. They create a special electrical attraction.

9. Engineers are people with scientific training who do what?
   a. eat pizza and sleep
   b. try to understand the universe
   c. plan, design, and build things

10. What is another word for the central problem of a story?
    a. conflict
    b. characters
    c. drag

Answers: 1. b 2. a 3. c 4. a 5. b 6. c 7. a 8. c 9. c 10. a

8467